# Cool
# Coyote Cafe
## Juice Drinks

# Cool Coyote

# Cafe Juice Drinks

## Mark Miller
### and Brett Kemmerer
### with John Harrisson

Photography by
Scott Vlaun

Ten Speed Press
Berkeley, California

1⊖
Ten Speed Press
Box 7123
Berkeley, California 94707
www.tenspeed.com

Distributed in Canada by Ten Speed Press Canada, in New
Zealand by Southern Publishers Group, in South Africa by
Real Books, in Southeast Asia by Berkeley Books, and in
the United Kingdom and Europe by Airlift Book Company.

Cover and text design by Rey International, Los Angeles.
Props and styling assistance by Trez Harrisson, Santa Fe.
Introduction by Fritz Strieff, San Francisco.

Library of Congress Cataloging-in-Publication Data

Miller, Mark Charles, 1949-
Cool Coyote Cafe juice drinks / Mark Miller and
Brett Kemmerer, with John Harrison ;
photography by Scott Vlaun.
p.  cm.
Includes index.
ISBN 0-89815-654-8
1. Beverages   I. Kemmerer, Brett.   II. Harrison, John.
III.  Cool Coyote Cafe Juice Drinks
TX815.M54  1997
641.8'7--dc21
Printed in Hong Kong

First printing, 1997

2  3  4  5  6  7  8  9  10 — 04  03  02  01  00

# Introduction

**Has anyone ever been able to resist sweet, juicy, perfectly ripe fruit? Wasn't the original paradise a lush garden laden with irresistible fruits. And, deep down, don't we all wish we could go back there? You can! Just pay attention the next time you're pushing a shopping cart down the juice drinks aisle.**

Just reading the names on the labels evokes a garden of earthly delights, where fruits of tropical coasts and mountain highlands blend innocently together: Guava Maya, Rain Forest Nectar, Fruit du Soleil, and Pear Divine...Mango Tango, Mango Fandango, and Hibiscus High...Mountain Apricot, Passion of the Islands, Maui Grove...Banana Casablanca, Pele's Papaya, Wild Tropical Guava, Hibiscus Cranberry...

The list could go on and on. A tidal wave of new products has hit the shelves lately; in fact, the beverage market is the single fastest-growing sector of the food industry. As these exciting new combinations make their way into the marketplace, everyday fruits like apples and oranges are being juiced and seduced by exotics from the tropics. Even Puritan cranberries have been lured out of boggy New England to intermingle shamelessly in multiple marriages with sensual mangoes, ravishing raspberries, and juicy, perfumed papayas!

**Do you crave intense, vibrant flavors and aromas? Thirst for cooling textures and sensations? Long for bright, intense colors?** Real, natural fruit juice drinks you make yourself (especially with tropical fruits) deliver everything you're looking for and more.

From amply stocked shelves and reach-in coolers, bewildering choices beckon—fruit-flavored spring waters, sodas, and wine coolers, fruit-flavored iced teas and coffees, and just about every kind of juice drink. They're all part of our speeded-up age of "smart drinks," smoothies, power frappes, and drive-through espresso bars.

On many restaurant menus now, you'll see a wide selection of nonalcoholic drinks—a far cry from when we were growing up, when you had to choose among a few fizzy colas and sodas. Back then, plastic beverage holders in cars were unheard of, not a standard feature, and no one would have believed that the sugar-propelled A&W empire would one day be felled by drive-through coffee stands. These days, the commuter has cup, can, or bottle at the ready, and the portable beverage has become a symbol of a lifestyle on the go.

But we want something else besides variety, convenience, and speed; we're thirsty for ever-higher flavor profiles and more invigorating sensory experiences.

Unlike their generic, processed, and oversweetened artificial cousins in the supermarket, the juice drinks in this book will envelop you in total sensory overload with their generous, intoxicating flavors; their irresistible variety of textures—slushy, smooth, frothy, thick, and pulpy; and their sparkling, jewel-like colors—glowing golden mango, vivid emerald kiwi, deep crimson cranberry...

We've always known that fruit is not just tasty, but good for us, too. We now understand the merits of rejecting processed foods high in sugar, fat, and calories, and want to get back to basics. We'd all do well to follow the advice of doctors, dieticians, and nutritionists, and eat more fruits and vegetables. These simple, unrefined, raw foods contain virtually all the nutrients we need—including vitamins and minerals, essential trace elements, and fiber. Fruits can energize us, strengthen our bodies, and reduce the risk of disease by boosting our immune systems.

These days, exotic fruits that we had barely heard of a few years ago are available in markets across the country, largely because shipping and refrigeration have improved, but also because fruit-lovers have arrived home from tropical moorings craving the flavors of their travels.

And fruits make delicious beverages. Alongside the old familiar standards—apples, bananas, grapes, strawberries—we now can try exciting, less familiar fruits, such as papayas, passion fruits, guavas, kiwis, and carambolas—not to mention tamarinds, papayas, pomelos, mangos, mangosteens, and guanabanas! With so many lavish flavors to choose from, there's never been a better time to start juicing.

While ripe fruit has probably always been the most healthful, natural, and universally enjoyed ingredient of all, many of the fruits available are still underused. Discovering different fruit flavors and experimenting with unusual combinations can open the gates into a whole new garden of fresh flavors. And one of the wonderful things about fruit juices is that they mix together so well that it's almost impossible to come up with a bad combination. Here's your chance to play mad scientist! Get the kids involved, and have some fun. The results may look a little strange, but chances are, they'll taste terrific.

**A Shangri-La of possibilities awaits you: zingy elixirs, seductive smoothies, jazzy coolers, festive punches, and a whole chapter of brilliant cocktails.** Best of all, there's no cooking involved, the recipes are short and easy to make, and the ingredients are inexpensive. So drink up, quench your thirst with cool juicy goodness, and enjoy!

# About Making Cool Juice Drinks

**Always use freshly squeezed juices whenever possible, rather than frozen or bottled juices. Not only are they more flavorful and likely to contain more beneficial vitamins and minerals, but they are also more acidic and less likely to be bitter or give drinks an off flavor.**

Always use superfine sugar when it's called for because it dissolves more easily than regular sugar.

For drinks that do not require ice (and even for those that do), chill the glasses. You can do this either by placing ice in the empty glass and then discarding it before pouring in the juice drink, or by placing the glasses in the freezer or refrigerator.

For blended drinks, ice should be crushed or cracked into small pieces so the blending process takes as little time as possible. Overblended drinks can be too cold. Ice for stirred drinks, on the other hand, should be in large pieces to prevent it from melting and diluting the juice.

The best way to crush ice is to place some cubes in a

clean dish towel or cloth and hit the ice on a solid surface or with a heavy mallet. For small quantities of crushed ice, you can cup an ice cube or two in your hand and rap the ice sharply with the back of a tablespoon.

Don't forget that fruit juice ice cubes are an easy and colorful way to dress up any drink. We've found that fruit juice ice cubes are always a big hit at children's parties.

**Measurements for Drinks**
**1 ounce = 2 tablespoons**
**2 ounces = 4 tablespoons = 1/4 cup**
**4 ounces = 8 tablespoons = 1/2 cup**
**8 ounces = 16 tablespoons = 1 cup**

To salt the glass, rub the rim with a slice of lime and dip it in a saucer of bar salt. Sugaring the rim of the glass is done just like salting. Simply rub the rim of a rocks glass with a slice of lime, then dip it in a saucer of superfine sugar.

Frozen strawberries are convenient to have on hand, particularly in the winter months, and they also help thicken any drink you add them to. We also recommend keeping frozen blueberries on hand as they make an excellent substitute for other berries in smoothie recipes.

While melons are nutritious and their juice is an excellent tonic, some people do not digest melon juice well when it is mixed with other fruit juices such as peach or apple.

Of course, you can convert many of the other recipes in this book into delicious fruit juice cocktails easily enough, simply by adding an appropriate liquor.

# Cool
# *Fruit Juice*
## Drinks

The recipes in this chapter will ease you gently into the art of making memorable fruit juice drinks. We begin with familiar and readily available fruit juices, such as

## orange, grapefruit, cranberry, lemon, lime, and apple cider,

letting them speak for themselves while giving their presentation a tasty or attractive twist. Then we graduate to more unusual but delicious juices and fruit nectars, such as

## mango, passion fruit, banana, black currant, and raspberry.

Most of the drinks in this chapter contain one or two fruit juices, but you should feel free to let your creativity and intuition direct additions or substitutions—especially if you have fruits you particularly enjoy or if you are fortunate to live in a city or region with a wide choice of exotic fruit. For example, balancing an acidic fruit such as citrus with a nonacidic one such as banana (or vice versa) makes for more interesting and complex flavor combinations, and thicker texture. Play around with the flavor combinations, have fun, and remember, your only limit is your imagination!

# Miami Sunrise

Bottled cranberry cocktail is sweeter than plain cranberry juice, which means you don't need to add sugar to the drink.

**Ice cubes**

**4 ounces (¹/₂ cup) freshly squeezed orange juice**

**1 ounce (2 tablespoons) freshly squeezed grapefruit juice**

**1 ounce (2 tablespoons) cranberry juice cocktail**

Fill a tall glass with ice. Add the orange juice, then the grapefruit juice, and top with the cranberry juice.

# Orange Blossom

These days, banana nectar is easily found in most grocery or health-food stores—one commonly available brand is Kern's.

**3 ounces (6 tablespoons) freshly squeezed orange juice or tangerine juice**

**3 ounces (6 tablespoons) banana nectar**

**1 handful crushed ice**

**Lime wedge, for garnish**

Place the orange juice, banana nectar, and ice in a blender and blend until smooth. Pour into a large wineglass and garnish with the lime wedge.

# Virgin
## Tamarindo

The tamarind tree, also known as the Indian date, is a subtropical species that yields pods containing seeds and a sour pulp. The concentrated paste made from tamarind pulp is a popular flavoring in Asia and the Middle East as well as Mexico. It's used not only in cooking but as a syrupy drink base. Tamarind paste is available at Southeast Asian markets.

**1¹/₂ ounces (3 tablespoons) mango purée**
**1 ounce (2 tablespoons) sparkling
mineral water**
**2 teaspoons freshly squeezed orange juice**
**1 tablespoon tamarind pulp, seeds removed**
**1 handful cracked ice**

Place all the ingredients together in a blender and blend until smooth. Pour into a chilled martini glass.

# Kona Sunset

With its tropical flavors, Kona Sunset will transport you to the Big Island of Hawaii, where they grow tasty strawberries irrigated with very cold water from thousands of feet below the ocean's surface.

**¹/₂ cup peeled, seeded, and chopped papaya**
**³/₄ cup sliced strawberries**
**Juice of 1 lime**
**1 tablespoon superfine sugar**
**1 cup sparkling apple cider**
**6 to 8 ice cubes**

Place all the ingredients in a blender and purée until smooth. Pour into chilled glasses.

# Almost

# Virgin Sea Breeze

Use ruby-red grapefruit for an even more intense visual effect,
and a splash of lemon-lime soda if you prefer plain
cranberry juice instead of the juice cocktail.

**Ice cubes**

**3 ounces (6 tablespoons)
cranberry juice cocktail**

**3 ounces (6 tablespoons) freshly
squeezed grapefruit juice**

**Sparkling mineral water or ginger ale**

Fill a tall glass with ice. Add the cranberry juice cocktail and grapefruit juice. Top with the mineral water.

# Cape Cod Spritzer

Cranberry juice cocktail is sweeter than plain
cranberry juice—your call.

**Ice cubes**

**4 ounces (1/2 cup) cranberry juice or
cranberry juice cocktail**

**2 ounces (1/4 cup) club soda or
sparkling mineral water**

**1 lime slice, for garnish**

Fill a glass with ice. Add the cranberry juice and top with the club soda. Garnish with the lime slice.

# Orange Pressé

Instant energy in the French tradition of *citron pressé*—freshly squeezed sweetened lemonade. Orange Pressé is an equally refreshing citrus drink that is usually made with thin-skinned juice oranges, which are specially bred to be sweeter and to yield more juice than common "eating" varieties like navels. Don't be put off by the juice oranges' uneven coloring and general ugliness—their juice really is much tastier than that of their more attractive relatives.

**Juice of 1 large juice orange**
**1 tablespoon superfine sugar**
**4 ounces ($^1/_2$ cup) sparkling water**
**1 orange slice, for garnish**

Fill a highball glass with the orange juice. Add the sugar and stir. Add the water and stir again. Garnish with the orange slice.

# Jungle Fever

Passion fruit, also called *grenadilla* (and *liliko*i in Hawaii), is one of the most aromatic tropical fruits. It can be found with increasing frequency in bottled iced teas, sodas, and sorbets. The passion fruit is native to the tropical jungles of Brazil. The mango originated in the jungles of India. Together these two tropical superstars make a lusciously smooth and aromatic juice drink.

**Ice cubes**
**3 ounces (6 tablespoons) passion fruit nectar**
**1 ounce (2 tablespoons) mango purée or 2 ounces (1/4 cup) mango nectar**
**2 ounces (1/4 cup) water**
**1 lime slice, for garnish**

Half-fill a tall glass with ice. Add all the ingredients, except the lime, and stir. Garnish with the lime slice.

# Grapefruit and
## Tonic

Tart and sweet, this nonalcoholic drink is the 90's alternative
to gin and tonic. Tonic water, also known as quinine water, was
originally made with a small amount of quinine extract, which
is obtained from the same South American tree that gave
us the cure for malaria.

**Ice cubes**
**3 ounces (6 tablespoons) freshly squeezed pink-
grapefruit juice or unsweetened
bottled grapefruit juice**
**3 ounces (6 tablespoons) tonic water**
**1 ounce (2 tablespoons) grenadine (optional)**

Fill a tall glass with ice. Add the grapefruit juice, tonic
water, and grenadine.

# Banana **Colada**

Here's a wonderful drink to accompany spicy meals, especially those made with the tropical ingredients of Caribbean, Asian, or Mexican cuisines. Or, enjoy it on the deck while you watch the sunset. Use light coconut milk for fewer calories.

**1 very ripe banana**

**6 ounces (3/4 cup) unsweetened pineapple juice, chilled**

**1 1/2 ounces (3 tablespoons) canned coconut milk, chilled**

**1/2 teaspoon sweetened toasted coconut, for garnish**

Place the banana, pineapple juice, and coconut milk in a blender and blend until smooth. Pour into a large chilled wineglass and garnish with the toasted coconut.

crazy for
coconut

# Sangrita

It seems as though everyone has their own Bloody Mary (or non-alcoholic Virgin Mary) recipe. Some like it spicy, others plain; some like garlic, some don't; some like plain tomato juice, others like multivegetable juice or added spices and herbs in varying quantities  This recipe, by our good friend Stephan Pyles, who owns Star Canyon restaurant in Dallas, derives its name from a contraction of the Spanish words *sangre,* meaning "blood," and *grita,* meaning "uproar." As Stephan will tell you, "If you want to increase the grita, add more jalapeños and Tabasco!"

**3 cups tomato juice**
**1/4 cup cocktail onions**
**2 small cloves garlic, chopped**
**2 teaspoons Worcestershire sauce**
**1 teaspoon salt**
**2 jalapeño chiles, seeded and chopped**
**1/4 teaspoon dill seed**
**1/2 teaspoon celery seed**
**3/4 teaspoon prepared horseradish**
**Juice of 2 limes**
**6 to 8 drops Tabasco sauce**
**Ice cubes**
**4 limes wedges, for garnish**

Combine all the ingredients except for the ice and lime wedges in a blender. Purée until completely smooth, about 1 minute. Strain and pour into tall glasses filled with ice. Garnish with the lime wedges.

# The Eggcitin'
## Egg Cider

The combination of cider, egg, and half-and-half is not only unusual but also a real eye opener. With a little added Calvados or apple jack brandy, it makes a fine hangover remedy in the tradition of "the hair of the dog that bit you."

**Ice cubes**
**4 ounces (¹/₂ cup) apple cider**
**1¹/₂ ounces (3 tablespoons) half and half**
**1 egg, lightly beaten**
**¹/₂ teaspoon superfine sugar**
**1 dash freshly grated nutmeg, for garnish**

Half-fill a shaker with ice and add all the ingredients except the nutmeg. Shake until foamy, then strain into a chilled martini glass. Garnish with the nutmeg.

# Merry
## Mangoberry

You can adjust the flavors of this creamy and delicious fruit drink by substituting other berries for the raspberries. Blueberries, strawberries, or blackberries—or even a combination—will do the trick nicely.

**10 chilled red or black raspberries**
**1 ounce (2 tablespoons) chilled mango purée**
**4 ounces (¹/₂ cup) half-and-half**
**1 teaspoon superfine sugar**
**5 or 6 ice cubes**

Place all the ingredients in a blender and blend until smooth. Pour into a large chilled wineglass.

# TomKat

This drink, for the adventurous at heart, is a great substitute for the traditional Bloody Mary. Some very tasty ginger beers are available at many gourmet food markets these days; Reed's is one brand of all-natural ginger beer to try. Ginger beers are spicier than ginger ale, but not as sweet.

**Ice cubes**
**3 ounces (6 tablespoons) tomato juice**
**3 ounces (6 tablespoons) ginger beer**
**Dash Tabasco Sauce, or to taste**
**Dash Worcestershire sauce, or to taste**
**1 lemon wedge, for garnish**

Fill a tall glass with ice. Add the tomato juice, ginger beer, and Tabasco and Worcestershire sauces, and stir well. Garnish with the lemon wedge.

# Bokan
# Dreamsicle

Dreamsicles, with their citrusy ice coating and creamy centers, were a favorite of ours when we were growing up. They're making a comeback, as you'll see next time you peruse the frosty cases at your local market. This is rumored to be an old family recipe of our onetime bar manager, Jim Kromer. It's even named after his grandfather (Bokan, that is!), so it must be authentic. Its flavors are reminiscent of the ice-cream treat that inspired its name. (See page 14 for photo.)

**Ice cubes**
**3 ounces (6 tablespoons) freshly
   squeezed orange juice**
**3 ounces (6 tablespoons) lemon-lime soda**
**1 ounce (2 tablespoons) grenadine**
**1 orange slice, for garnish**
**1 maraschino cherry, for garnish**

Fill a large wineglass with ice. Add the orange juice, the lemon-lime soda, and then the grenadine. Garnish with the orange slice and cherry.

# The Dark Banana

This drink is especially soothing as a midnight snack. Bananas and chocolate are marvelous flavor companions that don't have to be confined to desserts, as this recipe proves.

{
**3 ounces (6 tablespoons) banana nectar**
**3 ounces (6 tablespoons) milk**
**1 tablespoon Hershey's Chocolate Syrup**

Thoroughly mix all the ingredients together in a tall glass.

# The Raven

This inventive and unusually hued drink really flies when it comes to flavor. Black currant juice is available at gourmet food markets.

**Ice cubes**
**4 ounces ($1/2$ cup) pear nectar**
**2 ounces ($1/4$ cup) black currant juice**
**Dash sparkling mineral water (optional)**
}

Fill a tall glass with ice. Add the nectar and black currant juice and stir. Top with sparkling mineral water to taste.

Re**fresh**ing

# Dixon
# Rose

This drink is refreshing beyond compare, especially on a hot and
humid day. The community of Dixon, for which it's named, lies in
the Rio Grande Valley, between Santa Fe and Taos. In the fall,
orchards in the area produce some of the best apple cider
we've sampled. Good-quality sparkling ciders are
available at most supermarkets.

**Ice cubes**
**6 ounces (³/₄ cup) sparkling apple cider**
**1 dash grenadine**
**1 teaspoon freshly squeezed lemon juice**
**1 apple slice, for garnish**

Half-fill a large wineglass with ice. Add the cider, top with the
grenadine, and then add the lemon juice. Garnish
with the apple slice.

Lively

# Liquados

and Luscious

# Lemonades

Stroll through any marketplace in Mexico and you will come across large, two-foot-tall ribbed glass jars resting on counters, carts, and food stands. These jars hold a rainbow of liquados—fruit-flavored, water-based refrescos that are the juice beverage of choice throughout Mexico. Usually, the jars contain large blocks of ice suspended in the

# watermelon-pink, bright orange, or carmine-red juice.

No two liquado stands are alike, which is part of the attraction. Some of the more elaborate stalls offer a dizzying array of liquados—mango, lime, coconut, guanabana, papaya, pineapple—and the colorful liquids are as much a sensory experience as the deliciously fresh flavors that are ladled out of the jars into large, thick glasses. Liquados represent the infinite variety and vitality of Mexican food and drink. If you go to Mexico, be sure to try the local liquados, since every region has its own specialty fruits and ingredients (most liquados in big city stores are made with pure water).

Lemonade is a north-of-the-border summer icon closely related to Mexican liquados. It's surprising that more restaurants do not serve flavored lemonades. At Red Sage, Coyote's sister restaurant in Washington, D.C., we serve ginger lemonade with a hibiscus float, for example. In the recipes that follow, we combine traditional lemonade with other fruit flavors. Using the same methods, you can take advantage of all kinds of other fruit—

# pineapple, mango, papaya, strawberries, kiwis

—enjoying whatever is in season and looks best at the market. You can also use frozen fruit and bottled or canned fruit nectars when fresh fruit is out of season.

# Liquado de Mango

Fresh mangoes give this drink a more concentrated flavor and perfumed "nose" than does canned nectar. In this recipe, frozen mango is also preferable to canned nectar. Peak mango season is summer through fall.

**3 ounces (6 tablespoons) mango purée**
**1 cup water**
**Juice of 1 lime**
**2 tablespoons superfine sugar**
**2 handfuls crushed ice**

Place all the ingredients in a blender and blend at medium speed for 15 seconds. Strain through a medium-mesh sieve into a frosty glass.

# Liquado de
## Naranja

For this south-of-the-border twist on OJ, experiment with different
varieties of oranges, but keep in mind that the smaller, thin-
skinned "juice" oranges will yield the most liquid.

**Juice and peels of 2 blood oranges**
**$1/2$ cup water**
**$1/2$ cup sparkling water or soda water**
**$2 1/2$ tablespoons superfine sugar**
**2 handfuls crushed ice**

Place everything in a blender and blend at medium speed for no
more than 4 seconds. (Overblending pulverizes the bitter pith and
creates a bitter liquado.) Strain through a medium-mesh sieve
into a frosty glass.

# Kumquat Liquado

The kumquat is native to China, where its gold-orange color symbolizes good fortune. It is the smallest of all citrus fruits, averaging about $1^1/_2$ inches in circumference. Kumquats are available mostly in the winter months. Their thin skin is edible, and their juicy flesh—tart and sweet at the same time—makes them perfect for liquados.

**12 kumquats, sliced in half**
**1 cup water**
**3 tablespoons superfine sugar**
**2 handfuls crushed ice**

Place all the ingredients in a blender and blend at medium speed for 10 seconds. Strain through a medium to medium-fine sieve into a frosty glass. Drink while still foamy and cold.

Foamy

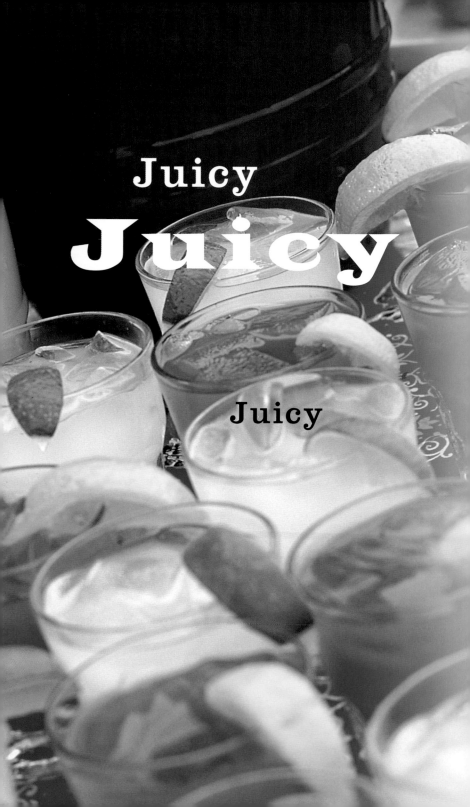

# Liquado de
# Limón

The citrus fruit of choice in Mexico is the *limón*, a small, round green lime, better known in the States as the "bartender" lime, similar in size and shape to the Key lime. The larger, lemon-shaped Persian limes common in U.S. markets tend to be more acidic, and their juice is less aromatic, so they are not as good for this recipe. You can, however, substitute ripe lemons, especially the sweet Meyer variety.

**Juice of 3 ripe Mexican limes**
**1 cup water**
**3 tablespoons superfine sugar**
**2 handfuls crushed ice**

Place all the ingredients, including the lime rinds, in a blender and blend on medium speed for no more than 10 seconds, until foamy. Overblending pulverizes the bitter pith and creates a bitter liquado. Strain through a medium-mesh sieve into a tall, frosty glass and drink while still foamy.

# Grapefruit
## Liquado

Grapefruit—*toronja* in Spanish—is a popular flavoring for drinks in Mexico. Its thirst-quenching juice makes us wonder why grapefruit sodas aren't more common in the United States. For a sweeter, brighter drink, use Texas ruby red grapefruits, or add a splash of grenadine and reduce the sugar.

**Juice of 1 large (or 2 small) grapefruit**
**1 cup water**
**3 tablespoons superfine sugar**
**2 handfuls crushed ice**

Place all the ingredients in a blender and blend at medium speed for 4 seconds. Strain through a medium-mesh sieve into a frosty glass.

# Liquado de
## Tamarindo

Tamarind is a popular sour-tart flavoring in drinks (including colas), sauces (including Worcestershire sauce), and Asian curries and chutneys. It is also particularly popular in authentic coffee-colored Mexican liquados. For more about tamarind, see page 17.

> **1 cup water**
> **3 tablespoons superfine sugar**
> **2 handfuls crushed ice**
> **2 tablespoons tamarind pulp,
> seeds removed**

Place all the ingredients in a blender and blend at medium speed for 15 seconds. Strain through a medium to medium-mesh sieve into a frosty glass.

# Liquado de Piña

Use freshly juiced pineapple for best results—the air-expressed Hawaiian fruit if possible. Pineapples are best when they feel heavy for their size and have an even orange-golden color and a strong perfume. However, I prefer the field-ripened, sliced pineapple in plastic bags (found in the refrigerated case of many supermarkets); it's far superior to under-ripe whole fruit.

**3 ounces (6 tablespoons) pineapple juice**
**1 cup water**
**2 tablespoons superfine sugar, or more to taste**
**Juice of ¹/₂ lime**
**2 handfuls crushed ice**

Place all the ingredients in a blender and blend at medium speed for 15 seconds. Strain through a medium-mesh sieve into a frosty glass.

# Coconut Liquado

Coconut milk—the liquid extracted from the flesh of the coconut—
is common to many cuisines, from Asia to the tropics of the
Americas. It's possible to make it yourself from fresh coconuts—
a good Asian cookbook will tell you how—but the canned version
is much easier to use and more readily available.

{

**4 ounces (¹/₂ cup) canned
sweetened coconut milk**

**1 cup water**

**Juice of 1 lime**

**2 handfuls crushed ice**

}

Place all the ingredients in a blender and blend at medium speed
for 15 seconds. Strain through a medium-mesh
sieve into a frosty glass.

# Liquado de Guanabana

The guanabana, also marketed in the United States and the
Caribbean as the soursop, is native to the American tropics.
The green spiny skin should be peeled and the dark seeds (which
are toxic) removed before the luscious, aromatic flesh, with its
flavors of banana, pineapple, peach, and apple, is juiced. This
deliciously creamy, sweetly tart drink is another popular liquado
south of the border.

**1/2 cup guanabana purée (from 1 or
   2 guanabanas)**
**1 cup water**
**2 tablespoons superfine sugar**
**2 handfuls crushed ice**

Place all the ingredients in a blender and blend at medium
speed for 15 seconds. Strain through a medium-mesh sieve
into a frosty glass.

# Papaya-Banana
# Liquado

The papaya is a luscious tropical fruit whose flavors peak when it's perfectly ripe. They are best bought slightly underripe—when they are a yellow color with tinges of green. In Mexico, papayas often have pink or red flesh, and some grow as large as water-melons. Ripen papayas at room temperature until they are a golden yellow all over, then use as soon as possible.

**2 ounces (¹/₄ cup) puréed papaya**
**1 ripe banana**
**1 cup water**
**Juice of 1 lime**
**2 tablespoons superfine sugar**
**2 handfuls crushed ice**

Place all the ingredients in a blender and blend at medium speed for 15 seconds. Strain through a medium-mesh sieve into a frosty glass.

# Strawberry
# Liquado

Strawberries have a wonderful balance of sweetness and acidity. They are common in milkshakes, jams, pies, and ice cream, but they also make a palate-pleasing, refreshing summer liquado.

**10 strawberries**
**1 cup water**
**2 tablespoons superfine sugar**
**2 handfuls crushed ice**

Place all the ingredients in a blender and blend at medium speed for 15 seconds. Strain through a medium-mesh sieve into a frosty glass.

# Frosty

# Willamette
# Raspberry
# Lemonade

Coyote considers himself quite an aficionado when it comes to roots and berries, and he'll tell anyone that will listen that there are more than two hundred varieties of raspberry—the most intensely flavored of all the berries—and the major growing area in the United States is Oregon's Willamette Valley. (See page 34 for photo.)

**1 pint (about 2 cups) raspberries**
**1/2 cup sugar**
**8 ounces (1 cup) freshly squeezed lemon juice**
**1 1/2 cups water**
**Ice cubes**

Place the raspberries and sugar in a blender and purée. Strain through a medium-mesh sieve into a pitcher and add the lemon juice and water. Pour into tall ice-filled glasses.

# White Peach
## Lemonade

Peaches come in many different colors, from gold and red to creamy white, and their flesh also ranges from golden to a pink-tinged white. Sweet white peaches are called for here, although the rich flavor will be just as delicious no matter what variety you choose.

**3 ripe white peaches, peeled, pitted, and chopped**

**$1/2$ cup sugar**

**8 ounces (1 cup) freshly squeezed lemon juice**

**$1 1/2$ cups water**

**Ice cubes**

Place the peaches and sugar in a blender and purée. Place the lemon juice and water in a pitcher and add the strained, puréed peaches. Pour into tall, ice-filled glasses.

# Blackberry-Apple Lemonade

In England, blackberries are commonly paired with apples to make the most delicious pies. This refreshing lemonade follows suit.

$3/4$ **pint (about 1$1/2$ cups) blackberries**
**4 ounces ($1/2$ cup) fresh apple juice**
$1/2$ **cup sugar**
**8 ounces (1 cup) freshly squeezed lemon juice**
$3 1/2$ **cups water**
**Ice cubes**

Place the blackberries, apple juice, and sugar in a blender and purée. Place the lemon juice and water in a pitcher, and strain the puréed blackberry mixture through a medium-mesh sieve into the pitcher. Pour into tall ice-filled glasses.

# All-American

# Lamy Lemonade

This hails from Lamy, a town just southeast of Santa Fe.
For how to sugar the rim of the glass, see page 13.

**3 cups freshly squeezed lemon juice**
**1 1/2 cups sparkling mineral water**
**1 cup superfine sugar**
**Ice cubes**
**4 mint sprigs, for garnish**

Combine all the ingredients except the mint sprigs in a pitcher
and stir until the sugar dissolves. Fill sugar-rimmed glasses with
ice and add the lemonade. Garnish each glass with a mint sprig.

SERVES 2

# Blueberry Lemonade

Nothing beats sweet blueberries and tart lemon juice on a hot day.

**1 pint (about 2 cups) blueberries**
**1/2 cup sugar**
**8 ounces (1 cup) freshly squeezed lemon juice**
**1 1/2 cups water**
**Ice cubes**

Place the blueberries and sugar in a blender and purée. Place the
lemon juice and water in a pitcher, and strain the puréed blueberries through a medium-mesh sieve into the pitcher. Stir well and
pour into tall ice-filled glasses.

# Chillin' Coolers and Peppy Punches

Back in the mid-'80s, wine and fruit coolers captured a significant share of the beverage market. Though their popularity has waned somewhat, fruit coolers remain a refreshing, flavorful way to enjoy fresh fruit juice. They satisfy the sweet tooth while filling the role of an "adult" drink. The coolers in this chapter are mostly mixed fruit juice drinks not at all dissimilar from liquados. They celebrate the bounty of summer fruit, and most

## get a lift from carbonated citrus-flavored soda or sparkling water.

Sparkling grape juice, apple cider, or plain water can all be used interchangeably where appropriate. So prepare your favorite cooler, head for the nearest hammock, and sip the goodness!

Fruit punches are fun to serve, and make picnics and gatherings more special. Originally, punches were a sign of opulence and were used to mark celebrations. They are still the drink of choice for large gatherings and special events, from wintertime eggnog and Christmas punches to summer rum and wedding punches. Punches are usually thought of as high-octane mixtures where ubiquitous slices of fruit float in a highly alcoholic liquid, often of inexpensive and mysterious provenance. But our nonalcoholic varieties offer the opportunity to

## blend fruits and juices to create deliciously complex and colorful fruit drinks.

Punches invite guests to help themselves, which has the added advantage of saving the host (that's you) all kinds of time and trouble.

# Bing Cherry and Vanilla Cooler

Coyote's favorite cherries are the dark red, almost-black Michigan Bing variety. At other times of the year, you'll want to use unsweetened bottled cherry juice, available from gourmet or specialty stores.

**Ice cubes**

**10 to 12 ounces cherries, stemmed, pitted, and juiced (about 6 ounces or 3/4 cup juice)**

**2 ounces (1/2 cup) sparkling water**

**2 drops pure vanilla extract**

**1 cherry, with stem, for garnish**

Fill a tall glass with ice. Add the cherry juice, mineral water, and vanilla extract, and stir. Garnish with the cherry.

Tangy

# Orange-Pineapple
## Cooler

Pineapple juice is a versatile component in fruit drinks. A splash of grenadine gives the cooler more color, or for added tanginess, add a dash of Campari.

**8 ounces (1 cup) freshly squeezed orange juice**

**6 ounces ($^3/_4$ cup) unsweetened frozen or fresh pineapple juice**

**4 ounces ($^1/_2$ cup) lemon-lime soda or sparkling water**

**Ice cubes**

**2 orange slices, for garnish**

Mix together the juices and soda and pour into tall ice-filled glasses. Garnish with the orange slices.

# Apple-Ginger Cooler

Freshly squeezed ginger juice really peps up plain apple juice, as well as other fruit juice drinks. To extract the juice, simply crush peeled fresh ginger in a garlic press. Alternately, use $^1/_2$ cup each of apple juice and a premium ginger beer, such as Reed's.

**Ice cubes**

**8 ounces (1 cup) fresh apple juice**

**1 tablespoon freshly squeezed ginger juice**

**1 apple wedge, for garnish**

Fill a tall glass with ice and add the apple juice and ginger juice. Stir well and garnish with the apple wedge.

# Plum-Cider Cooler

Juicy, ripe plums somehow define summer fruit. In Santa Fe, we're fortunate to have wonderful plum orchards in the fertile mountain valleys to the north. Plum juice and apple juice are a wonderful combination.

**Ice cubes**

**4 small plums, pitted and puréed**

**6 ounces (³/₄ cup) fresh apple cider or sparkling apple cider**

**1 apple slice, for garnish**

Fill a cocktail shaker with ice cubes and add the plum purée and apple cider. Shake well and strain into a chilled large wineglass. Garnish with the apple slice.

# Kiwi Kooler

Kiwis were developed commercially in New Zealand from the less flavorful, smaller Chinese gooseberry. (See page 54 for photo.)

**4 kiwifruits, peeled and chopped**
**Ice cubes**
**4 ounces (1/2 cup) unsweetened white grape juice or lemon-lime soda**
**Juice of 1 orange**

Pulse the kiwis in a blender or food processor until smooth, then strain the juice, pushing down to extract as much liquid as possible. Fill a tall glass with ice and add the strained kiwi juice. Add the grape juice and orange juice and stir.

# The Coyote Cooler

This is one of the Coyote Cantina's signature drinks. Add a little rum (use light or dark) to make an extraordinary cocktail.

**Ice cubes**
**2 ounces (1/4 cup) freshly squeezed orange juice**
**2 ounces (1/4 cup) freshly squeezed lemon juice**
**2 ounces (1/4 cup) freshly squeezed lime juice**
**2 ounces (1/4 cup) club soda or sparkling water**
**1 dash grenadine**

Fill a tall glass with ice. Add the orange, lemon, and lime juices and stir. Top with the club soda and grenadine.

# Summer
# Nectarine Cooler

Nectarines are firmer than peaches and more acidic. They are often sold underripe, so let them ripen at room temperature if necessary, until the flesh gives a little to the touch and they become fragrant. You can substitute peaches or apricots in this recipe.

**2 nectarines, pitted and chopped**
**4 ounces (¹/₂ cup) freshly squeezed orange juice**
**Ice cubes**
**4 ounces (¹/₂ cup) lemon-lime soda,**
  **or more to taste**
**2 ounces (¹/₂ cup) grapefruit juice**
**2 lime wedges, for garnish**

Juice the nectarines or purée in a blender or food processor with the orange juice until smooth, then strain the juice. Fill a tall glass with ice and add the strained nectarine juice. Add the lemon-lime soda and grapefruit juice, and stir thoroughly. Garnish with the lime wedges.

# Guajava Refresher

This cooling drink is named for the guava's rather lyrical Latin botanical name, *Psidium guajava*. Native to Brazil, the guava has green, yellow, white, or pink skin—the yellow ones are the sweetest. The flesh of the guavas available in the United States is usually pink, so the cranberry juice in this recipe intensifies the drink's visual impact.

**Ice cubes**
**1 guava, peeled and puréed**
**4 ounces (¹/₂ cup) lemon-lime soda**
**2 ounces (¹/₄ cup) cranberry juice**
**1 lime wedge, for garnish**

Fill a cocktail shaker with ice and add all the ingredients except the line. Shake well and strain into a chilled tall glass. Garnish with the lime wedge.

# Watermelon Cooler

Watermelon juice is naturally sweet and thirst-quenching. Either process the flesh through a juicer after removing the seeds, or blend and strain it.

**Ice cubes**

**6 ounces (3/4 cup) freshly squeezed watermelon juice**

**Juice of 1 lime**

**1 teaspoon superfine sugar, or to taste**

**1 lime wedge, for garnish (optional)**

Half-fill a tall glass with ice cubes. (You can also serve the drink without ice; just used chilled glasses and chill the watermelon juice.) Add the watermelon juice, lime juice, and sugar, and stir to dissolve the sugar. Garnish with the lime wedge.

Variation: Half-fill a shaker with ice. Add the watermelon juice, lime juice, and sugar, and shake until chilled. Strain into a Champagne flute or chilled martini glass.

# Cooling

Peachy

# Summer Fruit 'n'
## Basil Cooler

It's unusual to find herbs in fruit juice drinks, but you may want to experiment after you've tasted this combination. The basil gives this cooler a hint of licorice.

**1 peach, pitted and chopped**
**Ice cubes**
**1 or 2 small Thai basil or standard basil leaves**
**4 ounces ($1/2$ cup) freshly squeezed orange juice**
**2 ounces ($1/4$ cup) soda water**
**1 basil sprig, for garnish**

Purée the peach in a blender or food processor. Half-fill a tall glass with ice and add the puréed peach, basil leaves, orange juice, and soda water. Stir, and garnish with the basil sprig.

# Passion Fruit Cooler

Ah! The luscious, perfumed, rich passion fruit—one of the world's true delights. Add a little superfine sugar if the passion fruit juice tastes acidic.

**4 to 6 passion fruits**

**1 bottle (750 ml) sparkling unsweetened white grape juice**

**4 ounces (1/2 cup) chilled passion fruit juice or nectar**

Cut each passion fruit in half, and place the seeds, pulp, and juice of each fruit in a chilled Champagne flute. Carefully add the grape juice and then the passion fruit juice, and stir gently.

passion

# Mulled Spiced
## Cider Fruit
## Punch

Fruit punches are usually considered summertime fare, but here's one you can serve warm in the dead of winter. You may prefer to tie the spices in a cheesecloth and remove them just before serving, making the punch easier to pour. Unfiltered cider is usually more interesting than apple juice because it is often made with a variety of fallen apples. Look for it in the refrigerated case of the produce department.

**4 cups freshly pressed or frozen,
  unfiltered apple cider**

**1 cup pineapple juice**

**1 cup freshly squeezed orange juice**
  **$1/2$ cup freshly squeezed lemon juice**

**2 cinnamon sticks**

**1 teaspoon allspice**

**1 teaspoon cloves**
  **$1/4$ cup superfine sugar, or more to taste**

Place the apple cider, fruit juices, spices, and sugar in a large saucepan. Bring to a boil over high heat, stirring occasionally to dissolve the sugar. Reduce the heat and simmer for 10 minutes. Strain the hot cider punch into mugs.

# New England
# Berry Punch

Cranberries and apples are classic favorites among New Englanders. In this punch, the sweetness of the cider balances the tartness of the cranberries. The raspberry sorbet float makes this a festive party drink.

{

1 1/2 cups frozen raspberries

1 1/2 cups cranberry-juice cocktail

1 bottle (750 ml) sparkling apple cider

2 handfuls ice cubes

1 pint premium raspberry sorbet (optional)

}

Purée the raspberries in a blender. Transfer to a large pitcher and add the cranberry juice, apple cider, and ice. Serve in punch glasses, topping each with a scoop of sorbet.

# Sparkling

# Sangria Juice
## Party Punch

Traditionally, sangria is made with red wine, fruit juices, fruit slices, and sometimes a liqueur. However, an equally refreshing and colorful punch can be made using purple grape juice instead of wine.

**4 oranges**

**4 lemons**

**2 cups unsweetened purple grape juice**

**3 cups orange-flavored sparkling water**

**Superfine sugar, to taste**

**Ice cubes**

Juice 3 of the oranges and 3 of the lemons and pour the juices into a pitcher. Cut the remaining orange and lemon in half, then into half-moon slices, and add to the pitcher. Add the grape juice, sparkling water, sugar, and ice cubes. Pour into tall ice-filled glasses.

# Lucinda's Guadalajara Punch

This punch—minus the tequila—is adapted from a recipe by our good friend Lucinda Hutson. In her festive book, ¡Tequila! she suggests serving the punch in a large glass jar to show off the colorful fruit.

**4 cups freshly squeezed orange juice**
**1/2 cup freshly squeezed lime juice**
**2 cups freshly squeezed ruby grapefruit juice**
**6 cups pineapple juice**
**4 pounds watermelon, cut into**
    **bite-sized chunks**
**1 fresh pineapple, cut into bite-sized chunks**
**4 oranges, cut into wedges**
**2 lemons, sliced**
**6 limes, quartered**
**2 ruby grapefruit, cut into wedges**
**3 star fruits, sliced into star shapes**
**Crushed ice**
**3 cans (12 ounces each) grapefruit**
    **soda (such as Squirt)**

Pour the orange, lime, grapefuit and pineapple juices into a large, wide-mouthed glass jar and add the sliced fruit. Chill in the refrigerator. Serve the punch in wide-mouthed glasses or bowls filled with crushed ice (in the Guadalajara tradition), adding a generous splash of lemon-lime soda and a straw to each serving.

freshly
squeezed

# Power
# Drinks
## and Fruit
# Smoothies

Smoothies and their cousins—milk shakes, malts, and frappes—are a uniquely American institution that evolved from the proliferation of the ice cream parlor. Smoothies have been further propelled into the limelight by the advent of thick, fruit-flavored diet drinks and shakes, and by the trend toward "breakfast on the go."

Satisfying textures and flavors are the secrets to the booming success of smoothies. These fruit-based blended drinks have greatly increased in popularity over the last few years. As more people recognize the many

# inherently healthful and flavorful

qualities of fresh fruit, thick fruit-based blended drinks—aka smoothies—have become wildly popular. They get their texture from blending fruit or fruit juice with banana, yogurt, or ice; this satisfying, filling quality contributes much to their success.

Smoothies are closely related to the newest of newcomers:

# power drinks, energizers, and smart drinks.

These are smoothies with one or more added ingredients, such as soy- or whey-based protein powders, spirulina powder, herbal extracts (such as liquid ginseng), brewer's yeast, wheat germ, amino acids, immune-boosting nutrients, and weight-loss or weight-gain formulas. (Though these ingredients are sold at health-food and fitness stores, you must learn how to use them properly before you try them.) In Mexico, vendors selling fruit drinks at market stalls and from storefronts will often blend bee pollen and other supplement powders into the juice mixture. (In the Yucatan these stalls and storefronts usually go by the name of "California," no doubt reflecting their perceived place of origin.)

It is important that you use only ripe or overripe fruit to make smoothies. This not only maximizes the fruits' flavors, which are at their peak

## when the fruit is ripest

and has the highest sugar content, but it makes blending much easier. Unripe fruit tends to taste undeveloped, green, and "stemmy" when blended.

We use lowfat yogurt in the recipes that call for it, but you can use nonfat or full-fat if you prefer. You can also substitute frozen yogurt and cut down on the amount of ice, or eliminate

the yogurt altogether. In this case, simply substitute ice—
which, when blended, acts as a thickening agent. You can
also eliminate the ice if you prefer your smoothies at room
temperature. Or, you can experiment using lowfat or skim
milk, soy milk, or rice milk. With all these recipes, you can

## intensify the flavor

of the drinks and enhance their presentation by serving
them with colorful fruit juice ice cubes.

You'll also find some vegetable juice drinks in this chapter.
Vegetables not only make delicious juices but are extremely
healthful: your body immediately absorbs the minerals and
nutrients they provide. Many people prefer to

## enjoy the goodness of
## vegetables by
## drinking them

rather than steaming or cooking them, ensuring that no vitamins or nutrients are lost during the cooking process.

# Hawaiian Smoothie

Hawaii is Coyote's favorite vacation spot, and this drink contains tropical fruits that grow all over the islands.

**1 ripe banana**
**$1/2$ cup pitted and chopped mango**
**$1/2$ cup seeded and chopped papaya**
**$1/2$ cup chopped pineapple**
**Juice of 1 orange**
**Juice of 1 lemon**
**8 to 10 ice cubes**
**1 pineapple or orange slice, for garnish**

Place the banana, mango, papaya, pineapple, orange and lemon juices, and ice cubes in a blender and blend until smooth. Pour into tall glasses and garnish with the slice of fruit.

# Pineapple-Strawberry
# Fluff

Pineapple juice is rich in vitamin C and potassium as well as enzymes, and it's low in calories. It makes a great base for fruit drinks, especially when combined with any kind of berry.

**12 ounces (1 1/2 cups) pineapple juice**

**1 pint (about 2 cups) fresh strawberries**

**4 ounces (1/2 cup) vanilla or strawberry lowfat yogurt**

**1 teaspoon superfine sugar (optional)**

**2 handfuls crushed ice**

**4 pineapple wedges, for garnish**

Place the pineapple juice, strawberries, yogurt, sugar, and ice in a blender and blend until smooth. Pour into wineglasses and garnish with the pineapple wedges.

Rich

&

Creamy

# Coconut, Peach, and
## Yogurt Flip

Flips traditionally contain egg and some kind of alcohol, but
Coyote loves breaking rules. Besides, the coconut milk and yogurt
give this smoothie a rich, creamy texture. In the old days, back in
Colonial times, making a flip involved dipping a red-hot poker
into the concoction. Don't try this at home!

**1 large ripe peach, pitted, peeled, and chopped**
**2 ounces ($^{1}/_{4}$ cup) sweetened
lowfat coconut milk**
**2 ounces ($^{1}/_{4}$ cup) vanilla lowfat yogurt**
**1 handful crushed ice**
**1 peach slice, for garnish**

Place the peach, coconut milk, yogurt, and ice in a blender, and
blend until smooth. Pour into a large wineglass and garnish
with the peach slice.

# Rise & Shine Tropical Power Smoothie

This is a good pick-me-up if you're on the go and need to refuel with a satisfying, tasty drink. It's also replenishing pre- or post workout. Add a little frozen vanilla yogurt instead of the ice, if you like.

**6 ounces ($3/4$ cup) freshly squeezed orange juice**

**3 ounces (6 tablespoons) unsweetened pineapple juice**

**$1^1/2$ ounces (3 tablespoons) coconut milk**

**1 teaspoon honey (optional)**

**1 tablespoon protein powder (optional)**

**8 to 10 ice cubes**

**1 pineapple slice, for garnish**

Place the orange and pineapple juices, coconut milk, honey, protein powder, and ice in a blender, and blend until smooth. Pour into a tall glass and garnish with the pineapple slice.

# Banana-Ginseng
# **Burst**

Ginseng, a Chinese herb that is believed to strengthen the immune system, is used as a general stimulant and tonic. What better way to take it than in this flavorful fruit smoothie?

**6 frozen strawberries**
**1 ripe banana**
**8 ounces (1 cup) apple juice, chilled**
**$1/2$ tablespoon honey (optional)**
**1 tablespoon liquid ginseng**
**2 fresh strawberries, for garnish**

Place the frozen strawberries, banana, apple juice, honey, and ginseng in a blender and blend until smooth. Pour into tall glasses and garnish with the fresh strawberries.

# Blueberry Power Smoothie

These days fresh blueberries are available even in winter, when the New Zealand crop arrives in the Northern Hemisphere. Brewer's yeast, which is nonleavening and so-called because it is used to make beer, is an excellent source of B vitamins and protein.

**6 ounces ($3/4$ cup) freshly squeezed orange juice**
**2 ounces ($1/4$ cup) pineapple juice**
**$1/2$ cup fresh or frozen blueberries**
**$1/2$ ripe banana**
**1 tablespoon brewer's yeast (optional)**
**8 to 10 ice cubes (optional)**

Place all the ingredients in a blender and blend until smooth. Pour into large wineglasses.

# Mango Fusion

This luscious beverage lets the flavors of mango take center stage. The lime cuts the mango's richness, adding just the right amount of balancing acidity. You can substitute papaya for the mango if you prefer. Use a light, neutral-flavored honey.

{
**2 mangoes, peeled, pitted, and chopped**
**Juice of 1 small lime**
**6 ounces ($3/4$ cup) vanilla lowfat yogurt**
**2 tablespoons honey (optional)**
**8 to 10 ice cubes**
}

Place all the ingredients in a blender and blend until smooth. Pour into tall glasses.

# Ruby Grapefruit and Strawberry Smoothie

Here's a tasty, colorful liquid refreshment that can easily be converted into a power drink with the addition of a spoonful of protein powder or wheat bran. Pink grapefruit juice is sweeter and less acidic than the white, but if it is unavailable, or if you prefer, you can use white grapefruit juice with a splash of sweetened cranberry juice. (See page 74 for photo.)

**8 ounces (1 cup) pink grapefruit juice**
**6 fresh or frozen strawberries**
**1 ripe banana**
**8 to 10 ice cubes**

Place all the ingredients in a blender and blend until smooth. Pour into tall glasses.

# Two-Melon
# Smoothie

In peak melon season, you may wish to make this a three- or four-melon smoothie, using different varieties, such as green honeydew, crenshaw, canteloupe, pepino, and clavillon (a rich honey melon from the south of France). The lime juice provides just the right counterpoint of tartness.

**3/4 cup seeded and chopped watermelon**

**3/4 cup seeded and chopped very ripe honeydew melon or canteloupe**

**Juice of 1 lime**

**4 ounces (1/2 cup) vanilla lowfat yogurt (optional)**

**3 to 4 ice cubes**

Place all the ingredients in a blender and blend until smooth. Pour into tall glasses.

# Red Currant and Berry Float

Be sure to plan ahead and make the red currant ice cubes in advance; they make this tasty smoothie striking. Red currant juice is available at gourmet and specialty stores. Purple grape juice ice cubes are also good.

**$1/2$ cup fresh or frozen raspberries**
**$1/2$ ripe banana**
**4 ounces ($1/2$ cup) frozen vanilla yogurt**
**8 ounces (1 cup) white grape juice**
**6 ice cubes made with red currant juice**

Place the raspberries, banana, yogurt, grape juice, and 2 of the ice cubes in a blender and blend until smooth. Pour into wineglasses and add a red currant ice cube to each drink.

# Peaches Galore Fruit
## Fuel Blend

Peaches come in two categories of varieties: clingstone and free-stone. Clingstones are used mostly for the commercial market, while most retail produce markets sell freestone peaches, which are easier to cut off the pit.

**2 peaches, peeled, pitted, and chopped**

**1 ripe banana**

**6 ounces ($3/4$ cup) freshly squeezed blood orange juice (or regular orange juice)**

**8 ounces (1 cup) plain lowfat yogurt**

**1 tablespoon protein powder (optional)**

**3 to 4 ice cubes (optional)**

Place all the ingredients in a blender and blend until smooth. Pour into tall glasses.

# Rainer's Chi-Chi

We've told you how much Coyote loves Hawaii. His favorite watering hole there is Roy's restaurant in Honolulu, where the barkeep, Rainer Kumbroch, has an impressive repertoire of fruit drinks and punches that includes this smoothielike cocktail. Rainer has been known to add vodka to liven up this drink, but it's equally delicious without.

**4 ounces (1/2 cup) Coco Lopez**
**3 ounces (6 tablespoons) cream or milk**
**8 ounces (1 cup) pineapple juice**
**2 handfuls ice**
**2 slices pineapple, for garnish**

Place the Coco Lopez, cream, pineapple juice, and ice in a blender and blend until smooth. Pour into tall glasses and garnish each serving with a pineapple slice.

# Norman's Fruit
## Batido

Batidos are fruit shakes popular in many parts of the Caribbean.
This recipe is from Coyote's good friend in Miami,
Norman Van Aken.

**1 cup fresh papaya, peeled, seeded,
and coarsely chopped**

**1 cup fresh mango, peeled, pitted,
and coarsely chopped**

**2 cups fresh pineapple, peeled, cored,
and coarsely chopped**

**2 small ripe, sweet bananas**

**3 tablespoons freshly squeezed lime juice**

**1 1/2 cups coconut milk**

**2 tablespoons superfine sugar**

**2 handfuls cracked ice**

Place the papaya, mango, pineapple, and bananas in a blender.
Add the lime juice and blend until smooth. Add the coconut milk,
sugar, and ice, and blend again until smooth. Pour
into chilled tall glasses.

# Emerald Kiwi
# Smoothie

Kiwis are raised in New Zealand, Chile, and California, which means they are available year-round. Their brilliant green flesh makes a beautiful smoothie.

**2 kiwifruits, peeled and chopped**
**4 ounces (1/2 cup) plain lowfat yogurt**
**2 ounces (1/4 cup) pineapple juice**
**1 tablespoon superfine sugar**
**3 to 4 ice cubes**
**1 kiwi slice, for garnish**

Place the kiwis, yogurt, pineapple juice, sugar and ice cubes in a blender and blend until smooth. Pour into a tall glass and garnish with the kiwi slice.

**smooth**

# The Vampire

Next time you visit Mexico City, be sure to visit La Merced, one of the largest and most remarkable food markets in the world. The variety and attractiveness of the produce—some of which is quite exotic—is truly extraordinary. In the middle of the market, close to the subway entrance, next to the wonderful market cafes, is a wonderful juice bar where the idea for this drink originated.

**3 carrots**
**2 stalks celery**
**1 beet, cooked**
**1/2 inch piece fresh ginger**
**1/4 cup water**

Juice all the solid ingredients and mix together with the water in a tall glass.

# Cucumber-Berry
# Juice

Botanically, the cucumber, like other squash, is a fruit, even though we use it as a vegetable (the same is true of tomatoes and chiles). The unlikely combination in this recipe proves that just about all fruit juices complement each other.

{
1/2 cup peeled, seeded, and chopped cucumber
1/2 cup frozen strawberries
6 ounces (3/4 cup) white grape juice
3 large basil or mint leaves
}

Place all the ingredients in a blender and blend until smooth. Strain into a chilled tall glass.

# "Orange You Glad You Made This?" Carrot Smoothie

Carrot juice is probably the most versatile of all vegetable juices. It's easy to digest and even children (well, most children, anyway!) like it because it's so high in natural sugars. Carrots are bursting with beta-carotene, which is believed to protect the skin from sunburn, as well as vitamins and minerals. If possible, buy carrots with their tops on, so you can gauge their freshness.

**6 ounces (³/₄ cup) carrot juice**
**6 ounces (³/₄ cup) freshly squeezed orange juice**
**8 ounces (1 cup) lowfat peach yogurt**
**5 ice cubes**

Place all the ingredients in a blender and blend until smooth. Pour into chilled tall glasses.

Carrot

Crazed

Juice

# Jolt

# Fruit 'n' Veggie
## Blaster

This mixed juice is a major immune-booster, crammed with vitamins, nutrients, and minerals. Oh, and it tastes pretty good, too.

**2 carrots**

**1 red bell pepper**

**1 jalapeño chile**

**1 stalk celery**

**1/2 bunch cilantro or parsley**

**1/2 apple**

**2 plum tomatoes**

**1 clove garlic**

**1/4 cup water**

Juice all of the solid ingredients and mix together with
the water in a tall glass.

# The Power Breakfast

This breakfast-in-a-glass will get you going in the morning, full as it is of carbohydrates, vitamins, and valuable nutrients. If you prefer, substitute an apple for the pear. Keep wheat germ refrigerated and buy it in small quantities from health-food stores with quick turnover, as it is prone to rancidity.

**1 cup freshly squeezed orange juice**
**$3/4$ cup very ripe pear, peeled, seeded, and chopped**
**1 ripe banana**
**$3/4$ cup plain lowfat yogurt**
**1 teaspoon pure vanilla extract**
**3 tablespoons smooth peanut butter**
**2 tablespoons wheat germ**
**3 to 4 ice cubes**

Place all the ingredients in a blender and blend until smooth. Pour into tall glasses.

# Citrus-Yogurt
# Supremo

This straightforward, zippy fruit smoothie gets the day off to a good start. If you feel like "powering up," add some wheat germ, brewer's yeast, or protein powder.

**2 ounces (¹/₄ cup) freshly squeezed orange juice**
**2 ounces (¹/₄ cup) freshly squeezed lemon juice**
**6 ounces (³/₄ cup) plain lowfat yogurt**
**1 teaspoon honey**
**3 to 4 ice cubes**
**1 orange slice, for garnish**

Place the orange and lemon juices, yogurt, honey, and ice cubes in a blender and blend until smooth. Pour into a tall glass and garnish with the orange slice.

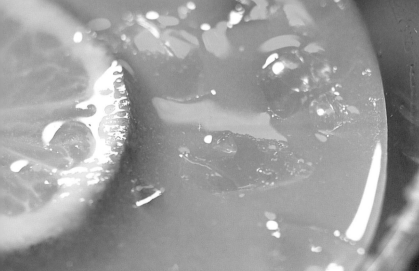

# Fruit Juice
# Cocktails

There is no substitute for the flavors of fresh juice—their tartness and acidity, sweetness and tang—and their complexity provides a wonderful, taste bud–rewarding partnership with liquors. Fermenting fruit is one of man's oldest methods of creating alcoholic drinks and spirits, so it is only natural to combine them with fresh fruit juice for festive, flavorful cocktails.

Cocktails are natural ice breakers that are sure to get any party going.

## The whirr and whizz of the blender, the aroma of freshly cut fruit,

and the colorful results make these tasty drinks irresistible.

As many of the cocktail titles in this chapter suggest, a drink can evoke a particular place, whether because of its ingredients (the Brazilian Daiquiri), geographic relationship (the Chimayó Cocktail or the Señor Playboy), or an association with a special location (the Playa Azul Piña Colada). One of the most appealing things about fruit juice cocktails is that

## they transport you to far-off places while you sip

them in the comfort of your own home.

In most of the recipes that follow, the amount of alcohol per cocktail is measured as $1^1/_2$ ounces, the equivalent of 3 tablespoons. This may seem an uneven amount, but it is the size of a standard jigger, the bartender's thimble or hourglass-shaped measuring device. If you use a jigger of a different size, simply adjust the other ingredients accordingly.

# Coyote's "Ultima" Margarita

This is our favorite way to start a meal or finish a long day. At Coyote Cafe we probably sell more margaritas than hot dinners. The popularity of margaritas explains why tequila has the fastest-growing sales of any liquor in the United States. Of the more than fifty premium tequilas on the market today, our brand of choice is El Tesoro *plata* ("silver"), a handmade, 100-percent blue agave tequila with a wonderfully refined flavor and smooth finish. When making margaritas, use fresh juice; never use bottled sweetened lime juice or sweet-and-sour mix. (See page 102 for photo.)

**1¹/₂ ounces (3 tablespoons) silver El Tesoro or silver Patrón tequila**

**1 teaspoon Cointreau**

**1¹/₂ ounces (3 tablespoons) freshly squeezed lime juice**

**1¹/₂ ounces (3 tablespoons) superfine sugar**

**Ice cubes**

**1 lime wedge, for garnish**

Salt the rim of a chilled martini glass (see page 13). Fill a cocktail shaker with the tequila, Cointreau, lime juice, sugar, and ice, and the same lime wedge, squeezed. Shake well for at least 30 seconds, until a foam forms on top. Strain into a blender and run at low speed for a few seconds, or just until the ice is cracked but not slushy. Pour and strain into glass. Garnish with the lime wedge.

# Sunburnt Señorita

Here's another trademark cocktail from Coyote Cafe. The bright
pink color of this watermelon margarita is reminiscent of the
vibrant pastel buildings of Oaxaca. (It's also the color of pale
gringos who've stayed on the beaches of Cancún or Cozumel too
long!) The intriguing, soft ripe flavors of sweet and juicy water-
melons capture the essence and warmth of summer in this
cocktail.  Always be sure to seed watermelon before juicing.

**1 ounce (2 tablespoons) Herradura gold tequila**

**4 ounces (1/2 cup) watermelon juice**

**1 ounce (2 tablespoons) freshly
squeezed lime juice**

**1/2 teaspoon superfine sugar or more, to taste**

**Ice cubes**

**1 lime wedge**

Sugar the rim of a tall glass (see page 13). Fill a cocktail shaker
with the tequila, watermelon juice, lime juice, sugar, and ice.
Shake well and strain into the glass. Garnish with the lime wedge.

# Mango Tango Margarita

Nature has outdone herself with mangoes, the king of all tropical fruits. There is no good substitute for the combined fragrance of bananas, pineapples, peaches, and citrus found in superripe, juicy mangoes. We prefer to use frozen mango purée in this recipe, or to purée the pre-peeled, chopped, frozen mango that's available in most supermarkets. *Añejo* ("aged") tequila is a "super-premium" liquor that must (by government decree) be aged, typically in oak casks, for at least one year. The tart lime juice contrasts with, and cuts, the richness of the mango, bringing out its full range of flavor.

**Ice cubes**
**1¹/₂ ounces (3 tablespoons) Patrón añejo tequila**
**4 ounces (¹/₂ cup) mango purée or nectar**
**1 ounce (2 tablespoons) freshly
   squeezed lime juice**
**1 lime slice, for garnish**

Fill a rocks glass with ice and add the tequila, mango purée, and lime juice. Stir and garnish with the lime slice.

super

ripe

# Chimayó Cocktail

The town of Chimayó, a 30-minute drive north of Santa Fe, is famous for its apple orchards, fall crops of red chiles, weavings, and *santuario* ("church"). This cocktail, made with local apples, is the signature drink of the renowned Rancho de Chimayó restaurant.

**Ice cubes**
**4 ounces (¹/₂ cup) fresh unfiltered apple cider**
**1 ounce (2 tablespoons) gold premium tequila**
**1 lime wedge**
**¹/₄ ounce (¹/₂ tablespoon) crème de cassis**
**1 apple wedge**

Fill a rocks glass with ice and add the apple cider and tequila. Squeeze the juice from the lime wedge into the glass and top off with the crème de cassis. Stir gently and garnish with the apple wedge.

# Sunrise Over the Mesa

This is Coyote's take on the classic Tequila Sunrise, and its name comes from the spectacular sight of bands of pastel reds, pinks, and oranges as the sun inches up over the mountains of northern New Mexico. In this drink, the varying viscosities of the liquids cause them to separate into distinct bands. The brilliantly carmine-colored grenadine syrup was once made with pomegranates grown on the Caribbean island of Grenada—hence the name—but these days it is made with other sweet fruit juices.

**Ice cubes**

**1 1/2 ounces (3 tablespoons) Herradura gold tequila**

**4 ounces (1/2 cup) freshly squeezed orange juice**

**1 ounce (2 tablespoons) grenadine**

**1 orange slice, for garnish**

Fill a large wineglass with ice and add the tequila. Carefully float the orange juice on top of the tequila, so that the two remain in separate layers. Carefully float the grenadine on top, in the same way. Garnish with the orange slice.

# Montego Bay Planter's Punch

Next to the sunshine, glorious sandy beaches, and inviting crystal-clear waters, the Caribbean's most famous attractions are its music and rum. Jamaica's Montego Bay ("Mo' Bay," as the locals call it) has all of these in abundance. If you're not planning a trip anytime soon, "no problem, mon" as they say in that Caribbean paradise. Just sip on this cocktail—it's almost like being there!

**2 ounces (¼ cup) light rum**

**1 ounce (2 tablespoons) dark rum, such as Myers's**

**1½ ounces (3 tablespoons) unsweetened pineapple juice**

**1½ ounces (3 tablespoons) freshly squeezed lime juice**

**1½ ounces (3 tablespoons) freshly squeezed orange juice**

**2 teaspoons grenadine**

**½ teaspoon pure vanilla extract**

**Ice cubes**

**2 dashes Angostura bitters**

**1 orange slice, for garnish**

**1 maraschino cherry, for garnish (optional)**

Fill a cocktail shaker with both rums, the pineapple juice, lime juice, and orange juice, grenadine, vanilla extract, and ice. Shake well and pour into a tall glass. Top off with the bitters, and garnish with the orange slice and cherry.

# The Unimpeachable
## Bellini

The Bellini cocktail was created in the 1960s by the Cipriani family, owners of the famous Harry's Bar in Venice, for one of the first revivals of the biennial art fairs held in the city. The bar, and the fine restaurant overlooking the Grand Canal, were made famous by Ernest Hemingway. The Bellini experienced a renaissance during the 1980s, and it's safe to say it has become a classic. The delicious sweet white peach purée can be bought in gourmet markets; Harry's Bar also markets a peach purée mix that's a fine substitute.

**2 ounces (¹/₁ cup) frozen white peach purée, defrosted, or bottled peach nectar**

**¹/₂ ounce (1 tablespoon) freshly squeezed lemon juice**

**4 ounces (¹/₂ cup) sparkling wine or dry Spumante**

Pour the peach nectar and lemon juice into a chilled Champagne flute. Carefully add the sparkling wine and stir very gently.

frothy

# Playa Azul Piña Colada

Along the sunny Yucatán peninsula of Mexico, south of the crowded beaches of Cancún, and not far from the spectacular clifftop ruins of the Mayan city Tulum, you'll find the quietly scenic beachfront town of Playa Azul, named after the turquoise blue sea there. Imagine yourself in just such a spot, beneath gently swaing palm trees, shaded perhaps by a modest *palapa,* overlooking the turquoise ocean as you sip on this tropical transport of delight.

**2 ounces (¹/₄ cup) light or golden rum**
**2 ounces (¹/₄ cup) unsweetened pineapple juice**
**¹/₂ cup chopped ripe pineapple,**
**or frozen chunks**
**1¹/₂ ounces (3 tablespoons) Coco Lopez**
**1 handful crushed ice**
**1 fresh pineapple wedge or orange slice,**
**for garnish**

Place the rum, pineapple juice, pineapple, Coco Lopez, and ice in a blender and blend until smooth. Pour into a large wineglass and garnish with the pineapple spear.

# Hawaii Kai
# Mai Tai

The Mai Tai cocktail was created in 1944 at Trader Vic's in San Francisco, one of the most famous cocktail bars of all. Vic himself was experimenting with seventeen-year-old Jamaican rum, when two Tahitian friends stopped by the bar. They tried this drink and toasted, "Mai Tai—Roa Ae!" meaning "out of this world—the best!" Thus the cocktail was christened. This version is named after the location of our friend Roy Yamaguchi's restaurant, Roy's, in the easten part of Honolulu. There's no better place to relax with a Mai Tai than on the outdoor patio while watching the sun sink into the Pacific over Diamond Head. Traditionally, the Mai Tai contains pineapple juice (which can be substituted here), but we've given this classic a twist by using passion fruit juice.

**Ice cubes**
**1 ounce (2 tablespoons) light rum**
**1/4 ounce (1 1/2 teaspoons) orgeat syrup**
**1/2 ounce (1 tablespoon) orange curaçao
   or Triple Sec**
**2 ounces (1/4 cup) passion fruit juice**
**1 ounce (2 tablespoons) dark rum**
**1 lime wedge**
**1 maraschino cherry (optional)**

Fill a large glass with ice and add the light rum, orgeat syrup, curaçao, and passion fruit juice. Stir gently, then float the dark rum on top. Garnish with the lime wedge and maraschino cherry.

# Sparkling
# Mimosa

Some prefer their mimosas with equal amounts of juice and Champagne, but Coyote loves to taste the bubbles. Be sure to use good-quality Champagne. Our favorite domestic bubbly is the Wedding Cuvée or Blanc de Blanc, made by Iron Horse Vineyards. The orange juice must be added to the glass first for the Champagne to keep its fizz. If you're feeling adventurous, add a dash of Cointreau.

**2 ounces ($1/4$ cup) freshly squeezed orange juice, chilled**

**4 ounces ($1/2$ cup) Champagne or sparkling wine**

Add the orange juice to a chilled Champagne flute. Slowly add the Champagne and stir very gently.

# Coyote's Sangria for One

We're fulfilling our social obligations by giving you the recipe for Sangria Juice Party Punch (page 71), a fruit-juice punch that serves a crowd. Now here's a recipe made of stronger stuff for you to enjoy all on your own.

**Ice cubes**

**4 ounces (1/2 cup) fruity red wine, such as Rioja or Cabernet Sauvignon**

**1/2 ounce (1 tablespoon) melon liqueur**

**1 ounce (2 tablespoons) freshly squeezed orange juice**

**1 ounce (2 tablespoons) lemon-lime soda**

**1 orange slice, for garnish**

**1 maraschino cherry, for garnish (optional)**

Half-fill a large brandy glass or large wineglass with ice. Add the wine, melon liqueur, orange juice, and soda. Stir gently and garnish with the orange slice and maraschino cherry.

# The Classic
## Screwdriver

The origins of this cocktail are a long shot from the sophisticated saloons and tropical waterfront bars that have spawned most of the classic mixed drinks. Reputedly, it was named by American oil-rig workers in the Middle East who stirred the concoction with the screwdrivers in their tool belts. For a variation, use a citrus or a spicy, pepper-flavored vodka to really wake up those taste buds.

**Ice cubes**
**1 1/2 ounces (3 tablespoons) premium vodka**
**4 ounces (1/2 cup) freshly squeezed orange juice**
**1 orange slice, for garnish**

Fill a tall glass with ice. Add the vodka and orange juice (add more orange juice to taste). Garnish with the orange slice.

# Blue Bayou
# Punch

Curaçao is a delicately flavored liqueur originally made from the peel of bitter oranges that came from the Caribbean island of the same name. The liqueur comes in a variety of artificially colored but useful decorative shades, from clear to blue.

**Ice cubes**

**1 1/2 ounces (3 tablespoons) vodka**

**1 ounce (2 tablespoons) blue curaçao**

**1/2 ounce (1 tablespoon) peach schnapps**

**1/2 ounce (1 tablespoon) Southern Comfort**

**1 ounce (2 tablespoons) freshly squeezed orange juice**

**1/2 ounce (1 tablespoon) freshly squeezed lemon juice**

**1/2 ounce (1 tablespoon) pineapple juice**

**2 ounces (1/4 cup) ginger ale**

**1 lemon slice, for garnish**

Fill a shaker with ice, and add the liquor and fruit juices. Shake well and pour into a tall, chilled glass. Top with the ginger ale and garnish with the lemon slice.

# The Apple of
# Your Eye

This recipe was inspired by a creation of the writer Michael
Jackson, an acknowledged expert on the subject of wine and
beverages, and author of *Michael Jackson's Cocktail Book*. For a
creative variation, serve the cocktail in a large, chilled apple shell
(Galas and Braeburns work well). Simply core the apple from the
stem end and scoop out enough of the flesh (reserving it)
so that the liquid will fit inside the shell.

**Flesh from 1 large cored apple**

**1¹/₂ ounces (3 tablespoons) Calvados
or apple brandy**

**2 ounces (¹/₄ cup) freshly squeezed orange juice**

**1¹/₂ ounces (3 tablespoons) freshly
squeezed lemon juice**

**Crushed ice**

Blend the apple flesh, Calvados, and orange and lemon juices
together, strain, and pour into a rocks glass filled with
crushed ice. Serve with a straw.

# Brazilian Daiquiri

This is a signature cocktail at Coyote Cafe, where a large glass liquado jar containing the rum, pineapple, and vanilla beans always graces the bar countertop. After the pineapple has marinated in the rum mixture and is strained out, it makes a real treat served with vanilla ice cream. If you're serving this for a party, increase the recipe generously because it always goes fast.

**8 ounces (1 cup) light rum**
**8 ounces (1 cup) golden rum**
**6 ounces (3/4 cup) dark Myers's rum**
**1 vanilla bean, split lengthwise**
**1 large, sweet ripe pineapple, peeled, cored, and cut into 8 pieces**
**3 tablespoons light brown sugar**
**Ice cubes**
**12 lime wedges, for garnish**

Place all the ingredients except the ice and lime wedges in a clean, large, ribbed glass jar. Cover tightly and let sit at room temperature for at least 7 days.

After 7 days, strain out the pineapple and vanilla bean. Transfer the rum mixture to a bottle and place in the freezer until very cold. Fill Champagne flutes with ice and pour in the drink mixture. Gently squeeze some juice from each lime wedge into each glass, then add the wedges to each drink. Alternatively, serve in shot glasses or martini glasses.

soothing

# The Fuzzy Navel

For a Fuzzy Pink Navel, substitute fresh ruby grapefruit juice for the orange juice. A closely related drink is the infamous Sex on the Beach, except that it calls for more than one fruit juice: simply substitute 2 ounces each of orange juice, pineapple juice, and cranberry juice for the orange juice in this recipe. And for Safe Sex on the Beach, quips Coyote, use the fruit juice mixture and leave out the alcohol.

**Ice cubes**
**1 ounce (2 tablespoons) peach schnapps**
**1 ounce (2 tablespoons) vodka**
**6 ounces (3/4 cup) freshly squeezed orange juice**
**1 orange slice, for garnish**

Fill a tall glass with ice and add the schnapps, vodka, and orange juice. Stir, and garnish with the orange slice.

# The Orange-Crimson
## Cranberry

This attractive cocktail gets its flavor twist from the subtle sharpness of the bitters. Bitters are made with distilled herbs and plants, bark, and roots, and they are often used as a digestive stimulant. Bitters are also what makes a Pink Gin pink.

**Ice cubes**

**3 ounces (6 tablespoons) cranberry juice**

**1 ounce (2 tablespoons) Grand Marnier or Cointreau**

**1 ounce (2 tablespoons) soda water**

**$1/2$ teaspoon Fernet Branca or Angostura bitters**

Fill a cocktail shaker with ice and add all of the ingredients. Strain into a chilled martini glass.

# Señor Playboy

Here's an old classic, a specialty of the Oriental Hotel in Bangkok, one of Coyote's favorite exotic watering holes. The Oriental is a great place to watch the sunset and the city's bustling waterways. The hotel's head bartender made a habit of regularly winning the city's competition for the best cocktail, and this is undoubtedly one of his finest creations.

**Ice cubes**
**3/4 ounce (1 1/2 tablespoons) Bombay gin**
**1 1/2 ounces (3 tablespoons) Cognac**
**1/2 ounce (1 tablespoon) Cointreau**
**1 ounce (2 tablespoons) freshly squeezed orange juice**
**1 teaspoon freshly squeezed lime juice**
**1 teaspoon fresh pineapple juice**
**1 1/2 teaspoons superfine sugar**

Half-fill a shaker with ice and add all the ingredients. Shake well and pour into a chilled martini glass.

# Index

Mark Miller is also the author of *Flavored Breads* (with Andrew MacLauchlan), *Coyote Cafe, The Great Salsa Book, Coyote's Pantry* (with Mark Kiffin), *The Great Chile Book, Mark Miller's Indian Market Cookbook*, and framing-quality posters featuring chiles and corn. To order, or to obtain catalogs of the complete line of books and posters from Ten Speed Press/Celestial Arts, call *1-800-841-BOOK*.